THE SECRET WORLD OF
Ants

THE SECRET WORLD OF Ants

Theresa Greenaway

www.raintreepublishers.co.uk
Visit our website to find out more information about **Raintree** books.

To order:
☎ Phone 44 (0) 1865 888112
📄 Send a fax to 44 (0) 1865 314091
💻 Visit the Raintree Bookshop at www.raintreepublishers.co.uk to browse our catalogue and order online.

First published in Great Britain by Raintree,
Halley Court, Jordan Hill, Oxford
OX2 8EJ, part of Harcourt Education.
Raintree is a registered trademark of Harcourt Education Ltd.

Produced for Raintree by Discovery Books
Editors: Kathryn Walker and Catherine Clarke
Series Consultant: Michael Chinery
Design: Ian Winton
Illustrations: Stuart Lafford
Production: Jonathan Smith

Originated by Dot Gradations Ltd
Printed and bound in China by South China Printing Company

ISBN 1 844 21583 0
07 06 05 04 03
10 9 8 7 6 5 4 3 2 1

British Library Cataloguing in Publication Data
Greenaway, Theresa
The Secret World of Ants
595.7'96
A full catalogue record for this book is available from the British Library.

Acknowledgements
The publishers would like to thank the following for permission to reproduce photographs:
Bruce Coleman Collection pp. 11 (William S.Paton), 13 top and 22 (Kim Taylor), 21 (Rod Williams), 30 (Stephen J.Krasemann), 32 (Luiz Claudio Marigo), 40 (Christer Frederikson), 41 (Gunter Ziesler), 42 (Kim Taylor), 43 top (Bruce Coleman Collection); Natural History Photographic Agency pp. 14 (Stephen Dalton), 19 (Anthony Bannister), 35 (Anthony Bannister), 36 (Kim Taylor) 38 (Brian Hawkes); Oxford Scientific Films pp. 13 bottom (Frank Schneidermeyer), 16 (Tina Carvalho), 17 (J.A.L.Cooke), 20 (Satoshi Kuribayashi), 23 (Satoshi Kuribayashi), 24 (Scott Camuzine), 25 (Tim Shepherd), 27 (Aldo Brando), 28 (J.A.L.Cooke), 29 (Mike Birkhead), 31 (J.A.L.Cooke); Premaphotos Wildlife pp. 8, 11, 12, 15, 18, 33, 34 and 43 bottom (K.G.Preston-Mafham).
All background images © Steck-Vaughn Collection (Corbis Royalty Free, Getty Royalty Free, and StockBYTE).

Cover photograph reproduced with permission of the Natural History Photographic Agency (Eric Soder).

Every effort has been made to contact copyright holders of any material reproduced in this book. Any omissions will be rectified in subsequent printings if notice is given to the publishers.

Any words appearing in the text in bold, **like this**, are explained in the Glossary.

Contents

Working as a team

Ants are insects. They have six legs and a body divided into three parts. Together with crabs, spiders, centipedes and other animals with a tough outer layer of **cuticle** and jointed legs, insects are **arthropods**. Ants are social insects, living in **colonies** that may contain many thousands of individuals.

Ants hatch from eggs into legless **grubs**. When fully grown, these turn into **pupae**. A pupa does not feed. Inside its tough outer case, the pupa changes into an adult ant. When this change, known as **metamorphosis**, is complete, the adult ant appears. Unlike many other insects, most adult ants are wingless. Only young **queen ants** and male ants have wings.

An ant's body is made up of a head, a **thorax** and an **abdomen**. An ant's head is equipped with eyes, a pair of long, jointed **antennae** or feelers, a pair of jaws and a mouth. Behind the head is the thorax, which has all six legs and, in the case of queen and male ants, two pairs of wings. At the other end of the ant's body is the abdomen. This is divided into two parts – a front part that is a narrow waist joined to the thorax, and a much larger

It has been estimated that there may be as many as 10,000 trillion ants alive at any time in the world!

The largest ant is the Bornean carpenter ant.

The smallest ants are tiny *Brachymyrmex* from South America and *Oligomyrmex* from Asia.

There are over 10,000 species, or kinds, of ant.

rear part, called the **gaster**, which contains the gut and other organs. Most ants have **venom glands** in their abdomens, and some kinds also have stings.

Most of the ants you see scurrying around are **workers**. They can run fast on their six legs and are able to climb rough vertical surfaces, such as walls and tree trunks.

abdomen
Some ants inject venom from a sting; others squirt it from the tip of the abdomen.

thorax
This is the middle part of the body, to which all six legs are attached.

jaws
These are sharp, so that the ant can bite enemies and snip up food.

mouth
Liquids and food crushed by the jaws are eaten.

antennae
An ant can smell and taste as well as feel with its very sensitive antennae.

WORLDWIDE ANTS

Ants live on all continents except Antarctica. There are ants in deserts, ants on high mountain slopes, ants in meadows, forests and gardens. Ants often get into our houses, schools and hospitals. Warmer countries have more kinds of ants than colder countries, but there is one kind of ant, *Leptothorax muscorum*, that even lives just inside the Arctic Circle.

THE COLONY

An individual ant cannot survive for very long on its own. It has to live with many others of its own kind in a **colony**. An ant colony is housed in a nest, where the young

Small, medium and large

Some **species** of ants have several different kinds of workers. These form sub-castes of different sizes, called minor, medium and major workers. Each sub-caste has its own job to do. Ants such as driver ants and leaf-cutter ants have large 'major' workers with especially big, sharp jaws that are called **soldier ants**. They guard the medium-sized workers.

I DIDN'T KNOW THAT

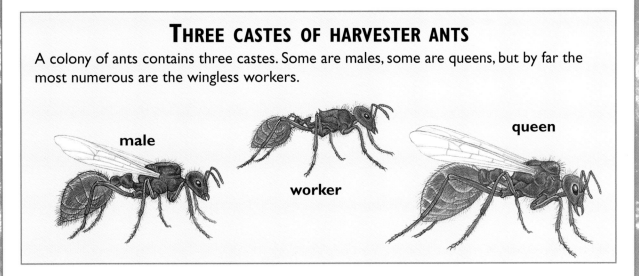

THREE CASTES OF HARVESTER ANTS

A colony of ants contains three castes. Some are males, some are queens, but by far the most numerous are the wingless workers.

male

worker

queen

ants are reared and where the ants return for shelter. Around the nest is an area, or territory, in which the ants search for food. The ants in a colony belong to groups called castes. Each caste has its own size. It also has its own role to play in the life and success of the colony.

CASTES

Most ants in a colony are **workers**. All workers are wingless, female ants. Although they are female, workers do not **reproduce**. As their name suggests, worker ants do all the work in the colony. They gather food, enlarge the nest, care for the eggs, **larvae** and **pupae**, and look after and feed the **queen ant** – their mother. To carry out these tasks, workers often have much larger jaws than other

castes. Worker ants of species such as the black garden ant are all about the same size.

Each colony has at least one queen ant. The queen ant starts a new colony, but as soon as her first workers appear, she does no more work in the nest. A queen ant is larger than her workers and the male ants. She has a large **abdomen** because in a healthy, thriving colony, she lays all the eggs. Although ants such as harvester ants have colonies with only one queen, colonies of wood ants and others may have more than one queen.

Male ants are usually smaller than the queen ants. They do no work in the colony. Their only task is to fly away and mate with young queens, usually from another colony.

Where ants live

We think of ants as living in the ground but, in fact, ants make their nests in many different places. Some spend almost their entire lives underground, rarely coming out into daylight. Many kinds of ants live in gardens and on farms, and are often seen running over paths or up and down walls. These ants, such as the black garden ant, nest near the surface of the ground. Others make nests above ground, in the treetops or even inside some kinds of plants.

An ant's nest is a complicated structure, with chambers, or 'rooms', at different levels. Ants use these chambers according to the time of day or the season of the year.

Leaf-cutter ants of the Central and South American rainforests make nests over 90 metres wide, reaching down to over 6 metres underground.

African weaver ants live in treetops. A large nest has been known to extend across seventeen treetops.

Tiny trapjaw ants live in small colonies inside split twigs.

A supercolony of **Japanese wood ants** covered an area of 273 hectares on the island of Hokkaido.

LIFE IN AN ANT COLONY

Worker ants keep eggs clean and stop mould from growing on them.

Worker ants carry pupae from chamber to chamber in their jaws.

The **queen ant** lays all the eggs.

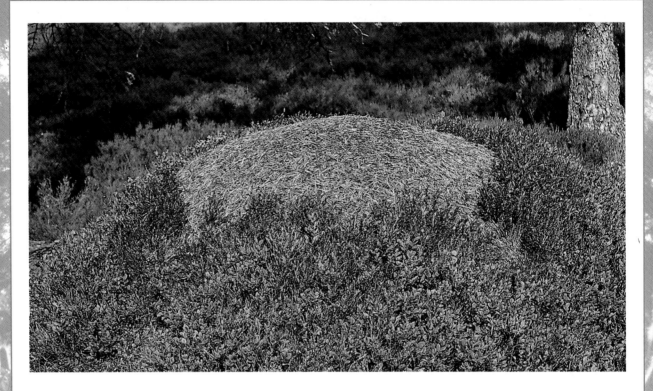

Wherever an ant **colony** is located, an ant's nest is highly organized. Eggs, **larvae** and **pupae** are kept in chambers connected by passages so that the workers can run from one part of the nest to another. Some kinds of ants make special chambers where they leave their rubbish. Ants need moisture to survive. Those living in hot, dry places make tunnels deep into the ground to reach damper soil. They also build tunnels that allow air to enter or leave the nest – a kind of air conditioning. At night or in cold weather, some kinds of ants block the entrances of their nest with pieces of bark, small stones or twigs.

Wood ant 'anthills' are enormous. It is best to keep clear of them because hundreds of wood ants will rush to attack an intruder.

ANTHILLS

The wood ants of Europe and Asia often build their nests around a tree stump. They make a huge heap, or 'anthill', of dry plant pieces, completely covering the stump. Underneath this, the ants dig chambers into the rotting wood and tunnels and more chambers into the ground below. In summer, it is warmest near the surface of the anthill, so the ants look after the **grubs** and pupae there. In winter, the whole colony moves back into chambers deep underground, where there is no risk of frost.

HELPING TO MAKE SOIL

As ants make their nests in the ground, they are always moving soil **particles** from place to place. Deeper layers are brought to the surface, and waste products from the ants help make the soil more **fertile**. In this way, ants play a part in forming soil. The harvester ants that live in the Painted Desert of Arizona, USA move up to 2.5 tonnes of soil per hectare during their nest-making activities.

LIVING INSIDE A THORN

The bull's horn acacia tree grows in Central America, and it has a special partnership with certain **species** of ants. Like all plants, its fresh green leaves attract caterpillars, aphids and other insects that feed on them. Fierce Aztec ants make their nests inside its large thorns. These ants kill any insect that lands on the acacia and feed the insect to their **grubs**. They also snip off climbing plants that try to grow over the acacia and keep the ground under it free from seedlings. In return, the tree produces fatty lumps at the tips of its leaves that the ants enjoy eating.

WEAVING A NEST

Weaver ants make nests inside a hole formed by the large leaves of tropical trees. Ants first pull up the edge of a leaf. Then they signal for more and more **workers**, who grip the edges of the leaf. Other workers grip these workers by the legs or waist, so that a chain of workers is made. The last of the chain holds on to the edge of another leaf. When two leaves have been pulled towards each other, another worker picks up a **larva** that is almost ready to **pupate**. When the larva

Like the Aztec ant, the acacia ant also lives in the thorns and stems of acacia trees. At the tip of most acacia leaves there is a fatty lump, which the ants eat.

or grub is squeezed, it produces a drop of silk. The worker carries the grub to and fro, joining the leaves with silk 'stitches'.

Weaver ant workers have powerful jaws that act like pincers, holding tightly to the edges of the leaves that make the walls of their nest.

I DIDN'T KNOW THAT

Chewed to a pulp

Carpenter ants are large ants that chew wood and other plant material into a **pulp** that is used to make the walls of their nest. In tropical forests, the ants use fallen branches as the building material for their nests. When these ants live close to human villages, they can cause a lot of damage to buildings by chewing through wooden walls, decking and wooden support structures.

Senses

For the ant **colony** to operate in a coordinated way, the hundreds or thousands of ants it contains must be able to communicate with each other. They have to work together to build the nest and all its underground chambers, tunnels, air passages and entrance holes.

Ants also need to recognize a threat and quickly signal enough fellow **workers** to drive away or kill the enemy. Any ant-eating **predator** that manages to break into the nest and eat the young ants, and maybe even the **queen** herself, may cause the end of the whole colony.

These wood ants are members of the same colony. They are communicating a message to each other.

Each species of ant is thought by biologists to have a vocabulary of between ten and twenty chemical 'words'.

Like dogs and foxes, weaver ants use their droppings to mark their territory. This warns weaver ants from other nests to stay away.

Wood ants can sense movements at a distance of about 10 centimetres.

An alarmed leaf-cutter ant makes a sound by rubbing a tiny ridged area of the abdomen against part of its waist to warn other workers of a threat.

Citronella ants make a substance that smells strongly of lemons from glands in their heads. This alerts other ants to danger and helps to scare off enemies.

Worker ants also have to find food, and male and queen ants have to be able to recognize each other.

Of course, ants cannot sit down and talk about things the way humans do, but their way of communicating with each other is quite amazing. Ants have senses of sight, smell, hearing and touch, and they can 'talk' to each other using chemicals. Ants release a variety of different substances from **glands** in different parts of their bodies, including their heads and their **abdomens**. Other workers can sense and **identify** these, so that they know whether their nest-mate is warning of danger or telling them about a new food source.

These weaver ant workers are working together to carry a dead insect back to the other members of the colony.

SIGHT

Like many other insects, ants have one pair of **compound eyes**. Each of these is made up of hundreds of tiny units, each with its own lens. Compound eyes are very good at sensing movement, but most ants do not have very good eyesight.

TWO QUEENS

If there is more than one queen ant in a nest, one queen challenges the other. She stands tall and threatens the other queen with open jaws. To avoid being bitten and killed, the second queen gives in by lying very flat against the ground.

This ant's **compound eye** has been coloured blue in this highly magnified (stereoscan) photograph.

each other with their antennae. An ant that wants to be fed by a returning **worker**, taps it on part of the mouth. This encourages the well-fed ant to regurgitate, or vomit, droplets of food.

CHEMICAL CONVERSATIONS

An ant's sense of smell is extremely important. The smelly chemicals produced by ants are used together to create many different meanings. Chemicals that are used to lay trails are produced in **glands** at the rear of the ant. Some of these show the way to a new source of food. Others indicate that the trail-layer has found a good site for a new part of the nest. Another chemical is used to warn ants that an enemy is some distance from the nest.

SENSITIVE FEELERS

On its head, just behind its mouth, each ant has a pair of jointed **antennae**, or feelers. These antennae are highly sensitive to touch, smells and even vibrations. When two ants from the same nest meet, they touch

Queen smells

Ants from the same nest can recognize each other by their smell. This smell is a mixture of smells from three sources. The most important of these comes from the **queen**. Her scent is spread all around the **colony** by the workers looking after her (as seen here – the bloated body is that of the queen). The second comes from the workers. Because they are all in such close contact, smells from the workers are spread from one to another. The third part of the colony's smell comes from the nest itself.

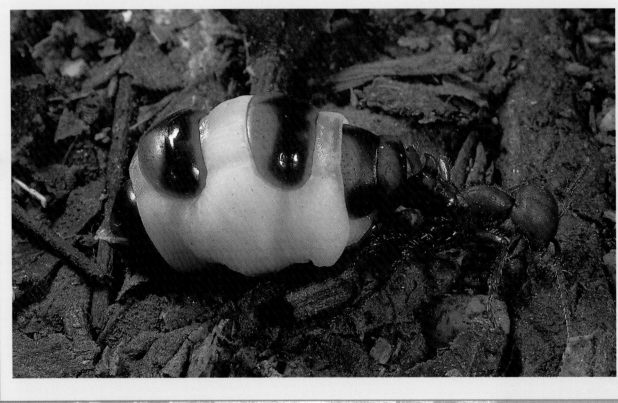

Alarm chemicals that alert nest-mates to an enemy close by are produced in glands in the ant's head. They work to alert other workers to help the first ant attack the enemy. These chemicals vaporize, or change to a gas, in the air, and are picked up by the antennae. One chemical sounds the alarm. The next tells the ants to run to the site of danger. Other chemicals encourage the alerted workers to attack and bite the enemy.

Food and feeding

Ants cut food into pieces small enough to chew and swallow with a pair of jaws, or **mandibles**. These can open wide or close tightly together. Different **species** of ants have jaws that are suited to dealing with different kinds of food. Most ants are **predators** that catch and eat other insects and **invertebrates**. By working as a team, they can overcome animals, such as centipedes, that are much larger than a single ant. A large nest of **foraging** ants helps to keep the populations of many kinds of insects in check. Some of these, such as leaf-eating caterpillars, are pests of farm crops and garden plants.

These driver ants are killing an assassin bug, which is itself a fierce predator of other insects.

A colony of wood ants can gather over 100,000 caterpillars in just one day.

The long pincer-like jaws of trap-jaw ants can snap shut in less than one-thousandth of a second.

A *Thaumatomyrmex* ant has mandibles with very long, thin teeth. It uses these to pick up and carry its prey, a very bristly kind of millipede.

Campanotus detritus lives in the Namib Desert, where it gets moisture when sea fogs condense on the sand.

Ants soon take advantage of a new food source. They will even enter houses to eat left-over pet food.

Ants also need water. In most parts of the world, water is easy to find, but in hot, dry areas, ants may have to travel some distance to find it. **Workers** of a large, hunting ant that lives in tropical America carry droplets of water back to

Droplets of dew are often the only source of water for ants that live in the Namib Desert of south-western Africa.

their nest between their jaws. Any water that is not needed by ants in the nest is used to moisten the walls of the nest.

SPREADING THE NEWS

If an ant that is out **foraging** finds a good supply of food, it eats what it can, then returns to its nest. To allow itself and other **workers** to find the new food again, it lays a scent trail from the food back to the nest.

FEEDING NEST-MATES

Worker ants looking after the nest and **larvae**, and the larvae themselves, have to be fed by the foraging workers. The hungry worker usually taps or strokes a worker that has returned to the nest until it is given food. The returning worker gives food by vomiting some of what it has eaten.

HONEYPOTS

In honeypot ant **colonies**, special workers called 'repletes' hang from the roof of their nest and are fed nectar by other workers returning from foraging trips. Eventually, they are so full that

Ants will share their food with hungry nest-mates, but only if the hungry ant makes the correct signal that it needs food.

The abdomen of each 'replete' is enormously swollen with nectar fed to them by foraging workers.

their **abdomens** are just swollen sacs. When food is short, the colony can survive on its own food supply. The bulging repletes regurgitate, or vomit, droplets of sugary liquid for the other workers to eat.

LEAF-CUTTING ANTS

All day, worker leaf-cutter, or parasol, ants climb bushes and trees, snipping out pieces of leaves and flower petals that they carry back to their nest.

Here, the pieces of leaf are passed to other, smaller workers called gardeners. The gardeners use the pieces of leaf to grow a special kind of fungus in underground chambers. The ants and the ant **grubs** all feed on the fungus.

Because leaf-cutter ants sometimes carry pieces of leaf high above their heads, they are also called 'parasol' ants.

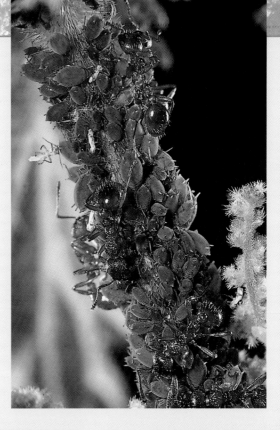

I DIDN'T KNOW THAT

Ant cows

Soft-bodied aphids, which are sap-sucking insects, drink sugary sap in order to get enough protein to grow. As a result, they produce droplets of strong sugary liquid called honeydew as waste. Ants such as the black garden ant and wood ant love this liquid so much that they look after clusters of aphids and stroke them to release more liquid, in much the same way humans keep cows to milk. The ants also protect these aphids from possible **predators**.

When it first hatches, the caterpillar of the large blue butterfly feeds on wild thyme. Then it crawls over the ground until it is found by ants that carry it into their nest.

CURIOUS PARTNERSHIPS
Some butterfly caterpillars have a strange partnership with ants. In Europe, the large blue and the alcon blue butterflies have caterpillars that feed on flowers for the first few weeks after they hatch. Then they drop to the ground, where they are found by certain **species** of **foraging** ants.

22

These ants carry the caterpillars, or **larvae** back to their nest. Here, both species of caterpillar actually feed on the ant larvae, but the alcon caterpillar is also fed by the **worker ants** as if it were an ant **grub**. In return, both caterpillars ooze out a sweet substance that the ants find very tasty.

SEED GATHERERS

In many dry parts of the world, including deserts, harvester ants collect seeds. They store them in nest chambers called granaries. Special workers with short but wide, powerful jaws crack open the seeds, and the softer parts inside are then fed to the grubs. Some of the seeds gathered by these ants are left uneaten. Buried in the **fertile** soil of the ants' nest, they can start to grow. So as well as eating seeds, ants also help to spread seeds away from the parent plant.

If this seed is not eaten by ant grubs in the harvester ant's nest, then it may germinate and grow.

Reproduction

When the time is right for ants to **reproduce**, the young, winged **queens** and the winged males crawl out of their nests and fly into the air. Males and females from the same nest are usually brothers and sisters. So that they mate with unrelated ants, all the nests of the same kind of ant in an area **swarm** at once. Suddenly the sky is full of flying ants. This means that there is a good chance that males and females from different nests will meet up and mate.

After mating, male ants flutter to the ground and die. The young queen ants also return to the

As winged males and young queens leave the nest, many workers also swarm out to protect them.

A queen ant mates just once. She then stores enough male sex cells in a sac in her abdomen to last for the rest of her life.

A queen leaf-cutter ant lays one egg every two seconds for up to ten years. During this time, she produces up to 150 million daughter worker ants.

Most queen ants do not survive long enough to start a colony. They are eaten by predators.

Unmated driver ant queens do not have wings. They have to wait for winged males to fly to them.

24

ground, where they bite off their wings or snap them off with their legs. The mated queen immediately looks for a good place to begin a new **colony**. She makes a small nest and starts to lay the eggs. While the first adult **worker ants** are developing, she has no help and so must look after these first eggs and

If more than one male tries to mate with the same queen ant, they all fall to the ground, where the males continue their struggle.

grubs herself. During this time, she does not eat. Instead, her now useless wing muscles are broken down to give her the food she needs to start her new colony.

FLYING FRENZY

Ants often choose a warm, **humid** day in summer to mate. As winged males and females leave their nest for the first and last time, hundreds of **workers** run around them. In the eastern USA, one of the most common ants is known as the Labour Day ant because this **species** always **swarms** around Labour Day – a US holiday on the first Monday in September. People cannot help noticing as hundreds of winged ants swarm out of cracks in pavements and lawns and take off to mate. Many of these mating pairs are eaten by birds and flying insects such as dragonflies. Others are squashed by cars or people's feet when they land on roads or pavements, or drown if they land on water. Only a very few of the hundreds of **queen** ants that leave a nest are successful in starting their own **colony**.

It's hard not to notice flying ants when they swarm out of their nests and take to the air by the thousands.

HARD-WORKING WORKERS

A queen ant lays hundreds, thousands, or millions of eggs in her lifetime. Each tiny egg is

For their size, ants can lift amazingly heavy objects. This ant is carrying a really large grub in its jaws.

looked after by worker ants, who keep it clean and make sure that it is kept at the right temperature. They move the eggs closer to the surface for warmth, or to deeper chambers of the nest if it is too hot and dry. The eggs hatch into tiny **grubs**, or **larvae**. Ant grubs cannot look after themselves. Worker ants feed, clean and look after them.

MOULTING

Ant grubs, just like adult ants, are covered with a tough outer **cuticle.** This does not stretch, so in order to grow, each grub has to **moult.** During moulting, the cuticle splits, and the grub wriggles out. Until the new skin hardens, it is stretchy. An ant grub moults three times, then it is ready to **pupate**.

EGG TO ANT

As the eggs are laid by the queen (1), they are looked after by worker ants until they hatch into grubs. These grubs are then fed and kept clean by the workers (2). When they are ready to pupate, some grubs spin **cocoons** around themselves (3). The young ants are pale and soft when they first come out from their cocoons (4) but soon become darker and harden.

I. **2.** **3.** **4.**

PUPATION

Ants with only one waist segment, such as wood ants, have **grubs** that spin a silk **cocoon** around themselves. Inside, the grub changes into an adult ant. Ants that have two waist segments, such as bulldog ants, do not have grubs that spin cocoons. The **pupa** looks like a pale adult but, with its legs tucked close to its sides, it cannot move. When the change from grub to adult is complete, the outer skin of the pupa splits, and a new ant wriggles out. The adult ant is full-grown, and does not **moult** again.

All fertilized eggs develop into female ants, either workers or queens. Only unfertilized eggs develop into male ants.

MALES OR FEMALES?

A **queen** ant is amazing. She decides which sex her eggs will be. At first, she needs plenty of workers, so she produces eggs that she fertilizes with the male sex cells that she has stored in her **abdomen**. These develop into female **worker ants**. As her **colony** grows, some of these female grubs are given extra food and are kept warmer than the others. These develop into new queen ants. The queen then lays some unfertilized eggs. These develop into male ants.

WHEN THE QUEEN DIES
Most colonies have just one queen. She is the mother of all the ants in the colony. A queen may live for many years, but eventually she grows old and dies. What happens then? Some of the workers may be able to lay a few eggs, but because these ants have never mated, the grubs that hatch from them are all males. Gradually, the workers die. The colony is doomed.

Pharaoh ant

This tiny ant originally lived only in the tropics but has now spread to many other parts of the world. It builds nests in heating ducts and hollow walls of houses, enjoying the warmth from the central heating. It is quite a pest! Queen Pharaoh ants have unusually short lives, just three months, but the young queens mate with males from their own colony. Each starts a new nest at the edge of the main colony, eventually producing a huge supercolony.

I DIDN'T KNOW THAT

A fearsome army

Army ants from tropical South and Central America and driver ants from Africa have a fearsome reputation for eating everything in their path – even human babies. Is this true? Actually, army ant raids travel too slowly to catch animals such as lizards, small mammals or people. However, a **swarm** of driver ants spreads out into a huge fan which is hard to avoid. Their victims are known to include a python that had just swallowed its **prey** and was unable to move quickly, a donkey and a gorilla. Even an unwatched human baby has been killed by driver ants.

When army ants are on the move, every living thing in their path struggles to get out of the way.

A 'raiding party' of army ants contains up to 200,000 ants and may be 20 metres wide.

The army ants move forwards at a speed of about 14 metres an hour.

African driver ants have the largest colonies of any insect – just one may contain over 16 million insects.

Driver ants are feared by humans because they have large, sharp jaws. Being bitten by hundreds of them at a time is a painful experience.

People leave their houses when army or driver ants pass through. They know that the ants will clear their houses of cockroaches and other pests.

Most of the animals killed and eaten by these invading ants are other insects, including other **species** of ants, spiders and other **invertebrates**. After a swarm has been through, the forest floor or grassland is cleared of almost all its ant and invertebrate life. The next time the army or driver ant **colony** goes out on a raid, it chooses a different direction. This ensures that the ants get enough to eat and that each raided area has enough time to recover before it is raided again.

CYCLE OF ACTIVITY

In the rainforests of South and Central America, colonies of army ants have a cycle of activity that lasts

Soldier army ants have extremely large, powerful jaws. Their job is to protect the **foraging** workers.

35 days. This cycle is divided into two phases. In the 'statary phase', all ant **grubs** in the colony **pupate**, and after ten days, the **queen** lays thousands of new eggs. During this phase, the colony stays in the same place, but raiding parties go out to bring back food for the ants looking after the queen, eggs and pupae. The new **workers** come out from their pupae at the same time that the eggs hatch into **larvae**. The whole colony then enters a second phase, called the 'nomadic phase'. The colony travels through the rainforest, making a new nest, called a 'bivouac', every night.

Camp followers

Many other kinds of animals follow the raids of army ants. The bicoloured antbird and the antwren (below) feed on insects that fly up to escape from the marching ants. Some species of rainforest butterflies follow behind to feed on antbird droppings. Other insect-eating **predators** stay near by to catch any insects that manage to escape from the ants.

Bivouacs are made on the side of a tree trunk or large branch. The bivouac is made by hundreds of **workers** clinging to each other's bodies. They make a kind of ant-basket that contains the **queen**, the **larvae** and the workers looking after them. If they cluster tightly together, the temperature inside the bivouac increases. If they loosen up, it cools.

RAIDING PARTIES

In the 'statary phase', raiding parties of army ants never cover the same ground twice. They travel in a slightly different direction every day. By hunting in such large parties, army ants are able to overcome entire nests of other ant **species**, as well as crickets, spiders and centipedes.

DRIVER ANTS

In Africa, driver ants also go out on raids. Unlike army ants, driver ants have underground nests. These nests are large,

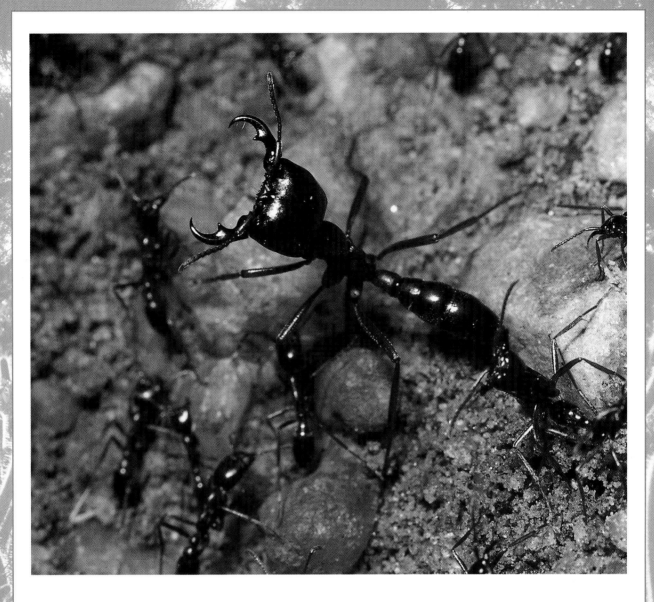

Soldier driver ants are much larger than the workers that they protect.

with a spreading network of tunnels and chambers hidden under the surface of the soil. Workers **swarm** out of the nest in a column that spreads out into smaller lines of ants, like the branches and twigs of a tree. At the front edge of the swarm, the ants kill everything too slow to escape. Ants snip off parts of their **prey** and carry them back to the nest.

All the flesh is stripped off a small mammal, leaving only the bones. As some workers leave the front line, they are replaced by others coming up from behind. After a few hours on the march, the ants turn around and swarm back into the nest.

Ant warfare

Ants are extremely aggressive. At the slightest threat to their nest, they spring to the attack. An ant attacks in one of two ways. It opens its jaws wide and bites, holding on to its enemy no matter how large. Then it swings its **abdomen** forward. Ants such as wood ants then spray a stinging, burning liquid from a **venom gland** into the wound made by its jaws. Bulldog ants, fire ants and others, actually have stings that they use to inject their venom. Although the effects of just one ant may be quite easy to ignore, the combined attacks of tens or even hundreds is not.

These two fighting ants are the same species but are from different nests. The loser will be killed and eaten.

Colobopsis ants in central USA and Japan have special large-headed workers that block the entrance to their nests so other kinds of ants cannot get in.

Workers of a Malaysian ant, *Campanotus saundersi*, have large glands that contain poisonous liquids. When these ants are attacked, they burst, covering their enemy with poison and killing themselves in the process.

Honeypot ant workers stand on top of pebbles with their legs stretched out like stilts, in order to seem larger than they really are.

Fire ants get their name because it feels as if your skin is on fire when these fierce little ants sting you.

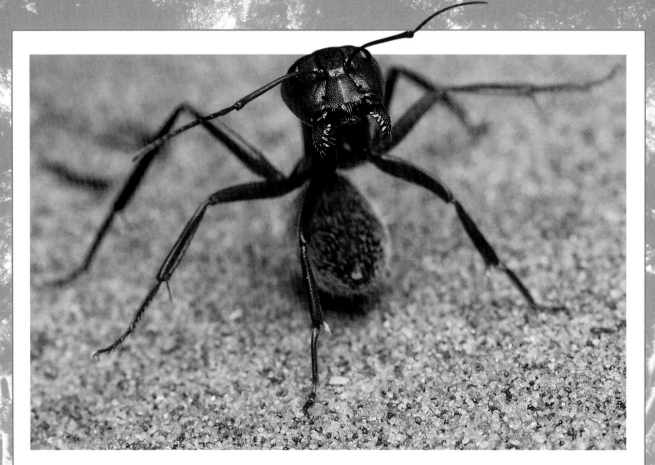

This desert ant is in the middle of an attack. It has bent its abdomen forward to spray stinging venom over its enemy.

Ants attack other ants – those of different **species** and even other **colonies** of the same species. Why do they do this? The main reason is that a colony of ants needs a large amount of food if it is to thrive and grow. For most ants that have a settled nest site, there is a limit to how far **foraging workers** can travel every day in their search for food. So it is important for them that all the available food should be theirs alone. They do not want to share it with other ants.

SMALL IS RISKY

A small ant colony is always at risk of attack from a larger colony of the same species. Workers seem to know whether a neighbouring colony is smaller or larger than their own. If they decide it is smaller, an all-out attack is launched. Ants kill each other by biting off **antennae** or legs, or by snipping each other in half at the waist. Those that sting do so in ant-to-ant conflict. The winning ants carry the dead bodies of the ants back to feed their own **grubs**. They may even raid the beaten colony, taking **pupae** and grubs back to work for them.

QUEENLY CONFLICT

Sometimes small groups of newly mated **queens** start a **colony** together. The advantages are that the colony grows more quickly than if just one queen sets up a home by herself. As these colonies with many queens grow, the queens begin a power struggle that results in the death of all except one. **Dominant** queens threaten the weaker ones, and the **workers** often attack and kill the losers.

Killer ants

The bites and venoms of most kinds of ants cause pain to people who are attacked, but are rarely serious. The Australian bulldog ant is an exception. It has a venom strong enough to kill humans who are allergic to it. Thirty stings may be fatal, and if you accidentally disturb a bulldog ant's nest, a lot more than 30 angry ants may attack you.

I DIDN'T KNOW THAT

HOUSE ARREST

Tiny *Forelius pruinosus* ants from Arizona, USA steal food from honeypot ant workers, and they can also stop the larger honeypot ants from **foraging** for food, even around their own nest site. Large numbers of the smaller ants cluster around the entrances of the honeypot ants' nest. As honeypot ant workers try to leave their nest, they are driven back by a chemical spray. Another related ant, *Conomyra*, drops a hail of tiny stones down the entrance holes, as well as spraying bad-smelling chemicals.

Raiding ants grab ant pupae in their jaws and carry them away. When these stolen workers come out they will work as slaves in the raiders' nest.

SLAVE-MAKING ANTS

Some **species** of ant workers are fierce fighters, but they cannot make nests or look after themselves. Instead, they raid other ants' nests, killing the workers and stealing the **pupae**, which they carry home to their nests to work as slaves. When the workers come out from these stolen pupae, they look after their 'masters', caring for their eggs and **grubs** and feeding the workers.

Enemies of ants

Left alone, most ants do little or no harm to people. Some kinds are so rare that they are hardly ever seen. Ants can be helpful, eating pests and improving the soil, but they can also be harmful, and many have painful bites and stings.

Ants become pests when they harm the roots of crops and garden plants by building their nest among them. Leaf-cutter ants are a serious nuisance on a

Fruit trees are sprayed to kill insect pests, but the sprays will also kill the ants that eat some of those pests.

Basiceros ants, which live in the American tropics, hide themselves from ant-eating enemies by covering themselves with fine particles of soil that get stuck on their hairy bodies.

Harvester ant workers keep spiders from catching them in webs by closing nearby nest entrances and staying inside.

A termite-eating ant from south-western USA goes out hunting only at a time of day when parasitic flies that would attack it are not active.

The ant-eating aardvark can close its nostrils to prevent ants from crawling inside.

The assassin bug can copy the scent code that ants use to guide nest-mates to food. It lays false trails and eats the ants that follow them.

tropical fruit plantation, where they strip trees of foliage. Sometimes ants enter houses and infest food stores or even chew away structural timbers. When ants do become pests, humans try to get rid of them, sometimes by using chemical **pesticides**.

Ants also have many natural enemies, or **predators**, that eat them. Although one ant is not much of a meal, a whole nest of

Leaf-cutter ants have stripped many of the leaves on this tree down to the stems. This can be serious damage on a plantation of tropical fruit trees.

ants, plus eggs, **grubs** and **pupae**, can add up to quite a feast. Even some quite large mammals break into ants' nests, and gobble up as many as possible. Birds, lizards and other insects such as beetles also eat ants, but for many ants, their worst enemies are other ants.

ANT-EATING MAMMALS

For the animals that eat them, it is vital that as many ants as possible are caught and swallowed before they scurry away underground, taking **grubs** and **pupae** with them. Mammals whose diet is made up mostly of ants and termites can do just this. Termites are not related to ants, but like ants they are insects that live in huge **colonies**.

Animals that specialize in eating ants include the short-beaked echidna from Australia, the giant

Armadillos eat ants as well as other insects and soft fruit. Scientists in Texas, USA discovered that one armadillo had eaten 40,000 ants in one meal!

anteater, tamandua and silky anteaters from South America, and the aardvark, which lives in Africa. Echidnas and anteaters are all toothless, but they have very long, sticky tongues so they can pick up lots of ants extremely quickly. The giant anteater, tamandua and silky anteater also have long, powerful claws to rip open ants' nests.

PARASITIC FLIES

A **parasite** is an animal that feeds on or in another living animal. As they snip up and carry home pieces of leaf, medium-sized leaf-cutter ant **workers** are at risk from parasitic flies. These flies need to lay eggs on the ants so that each of their own grubs can feed and develop inside a worker ant. To stop this, tiny leaf-cutter workers, called minims, ride on the pieces of leaf and attack any parasitic fly that comes too near.

The extraordinarily long, sticky tongue of the silky anteater is ideal for catching ants as they try to escape from the tree nest that the anteater has just ripped open.

ANT-EATING BIRDS

Birds that peck up ants seem able to stand the bites and stings of their **prey**. In Europe, the green woodpecker spends much of its time on the ground eating ants, even stabbing its beak into large wood ant mounds!

In the USA, the common flicker is a woodpecker that does much the same thing.

When flying male and female ants take off on their mating flight, ant-eating birds, such as swifts and fly-catchers, are ready and waiting to catch them in the air. On the ground, pheasants, hens and partridges are among the many other kinds of birds that peck up the newly mated **queens** as they return to the ground and shed their wings.

UNINVITED GUESTS

The moth-butterfly caterpillar of Australia catches and eats weaver ant **grubs**, and the **workers** are powerless to stop it. The caterpillar has a leathery, shield-like back. It clings very tightly to the leafy wall of the weaver ant's nest. When it is hungry, it raises itself slightly and swamps a number of ant grubs. Then it clamps down hard and eats them. Ants cannot bite through or wriggle under this tough shield.

Like most woodpeckers, the green woodpecker eats many kinds of insects, but this **species** is particularly fond of ants. It strikes into an ant's nest on the ground with its beak and picks up the ants with its long, sticky tongue.

Tasty!

In some parts of the world, people eat ants. Weaver ants are eaten in some parts of the Philippines, and honeypot ants are dug up by Australian aborigines. The sugary liquid that each replete (see pages 20-21) contains is very similar to honey. Different kinds of honeypot ants are collected and eaten by people in rural parts of Mexico.

THE FUTURE OF ANTS

Ants and their skill for social organization are among the most fascinating aspects of the natural world. A lot is now known about the lives of many different kinds of ants, but there is still much more to be discovered about the rest. It is important to conserve the **habitats** in which they live, especially those of the rarest and most specialized kinds.

This ant is in an alert position in its rainforest home in Trinidad. People also have to stay alert – to make sure that rainforests all around the world are conserved for ants and other wildlife.

Glossary

abdomen back part of an ant's body, made up of a narrow waist and a gaster

antennae pair of jointed 'feelers' on the head of the ant, which are highly sensitive to touch, smell and vibration

arthropod invertebrate animal that has a tough outer layer called a cuticle, or exoskeleton, and jointed legs

cocoon silk case that some kinds of ant larvae spin around themselves before pupating

colony large number of animals of the same species, living closely together

compound eye eye made up of hundreds of tiny units, each with its own lens

cuticle tough outer layer, or exoskeleton, of an arthropod that supports and protects the body within it

dominant superior or most powerful

fertile capable of reproducing or producing a lot

forage to search for food

gaster rear part of the ant's abdomen that contains the gut and other organs

gland organ in an animal's body that produces specific substances

grub worm-like larval stage of an ant's life cycle after it has hatched

habitat natural home of an animal or plant

humid moist or damp

identify to recognize or know what something is

invertebrate animal that does not have a backbone

larva (plural: **larvae**) stage in the life cycle of an animal that hatches from an egg but has not yet reached adult form

mandibles pair of jaws

metamorphosis change from pupa to adult ant

moult to shed the entire outer layer of skin

parasite animal that feeds on or in another animal

particles very tiny pieces

pesticides substances that people use to kill off creatures that they find troublesome or destructive

predator animal that hunts another animal for food

prey animal that is caught and eaten by another animal

pulp moist, soft substance

pupa (plural: **pupae**) stage in the life cycle of an ant when it changes from a larva into an adult

queen ant female ant that mates with a male and then lays all the eggs in an ant colony

reproduce to have or give birth to young

soldier ant worker ant that is larger than the other workers, and whose job it is to defend the ant colony

species kind of animal

swarm movement of a colony or large group of ants

thorax middle part of an ant's body to which the legs are attached

venom poisonous liquid injected into the body of another animal through stings, fangs or claws

worker ant wingless female ant that does not reproduce but looks after the young ants, collects food and keeps the nest clean

Further information

Books

Animal Groups: Life in a Colony: Ants, Richard and Louise Spilsbury (Heinemann Library, 2003)

Ants, Ray North (Whittet Books, 1996)

Collins Field Guide: Insects of Britain and Northern Europe (Collins, 1993)

Keeping Minibeasts: Ants, Barrie Watts (Franklin Watts, 2003)

Minibeast Pets: Ants, Theresa Greenaway (Hodder Wayland, 2000)

Websites

Myrmecology: The Scientific Study of Ants
www.myrmecology.org
Information and scientific facts about ants. Contains material about classification, colony founding, nest building, and foraging strategies. Also offers tips and guidelines for building artificial nests and starting ant colonies at home.

Index

Numbers in *italic* indicate pictures